someecards

The Official Compendium of Snark

The Official Compendium of Snark

The best quips, witticisms, and
inappropriate words for every occasion

FALL RIVER PRESS

New York

FALL RIVER PRESS

New York

An Imprint of Sterling Publishing
1166 Avenue of the Americas
New York, NY 10036

FALL RIVER PRESS and the distinctive Fall River Press logo
are registered trademarks of Barnes & Noble, Inc.

This 2015 edition is a compilation of the following books:

If You Don't Love Books, You're Going to Love This Book (someecards):
45 Cards for All Occasions, from Extremely Important to Utterly Pointless,
© 2009 by Duncan Mitchell and Brook Lundy

You'll Love This Book as Much as You Hate Your Job (someecards):
45 Cards for Decorating Your Cubicle, Insulting Coworkers, and Justifying Your
Excessive Drinking. © 2011 by Duncan Mitchell and Brook Lundy

If You Read Anything Offline This Year, Make It This Book (someecards):
45 Ways to Tell People You're Taking a Momentary Break from the Internet,
© 2013 by Duncan Mitchell and Brook Lundy

ISBN 978-1-4351-6113-9

For information about custom editions, special sales, and premium and corporate purchases, please
contact Sterling Special Sales at 800-805-5489 or specialsales@sterlingpublishing.com.

Manufactured in China

4 6 8 10 9 7 5 3

www.sterlingpublishing.com

someecards.com

Contents

INTRODUCTION   7
BIRTHDAY   9
APOLOGY   27
ANNIVERSARY   31
CONGRATULATIONS   38
MOTHER'S DAY   45
BABY   49
FATHER'S DAY   52
GET WELL   55
GRADUATION   60
WEDDING   65
THANKS   71
COURTESY HELLO   75
FRIENDSHIP   77
ENCOURAGEMENT   85
FYI   89
WORK   93
FAREWELL   126
ABOUT THE AUTHORS   128

Introduction

If you like someecards.com, you're going to feel exactly the same or even better about this best-of collection of perfect sentiments for every occasion. Use these sayings at any gathering or for any special event, and you'll look even more thoughtful, witty, caring, or obnoxious than you may already be!

There are many occasions where the right phrase or quip can come in handy, for example: do you want to wish someone well on their new job, but you know, deep down, that they're just not that into it? See page 38. If you find it difficult to express the proper emotion for a birthday, look no further than page 11. Wish the bride and groom well on page 66, and see how to reveal your true value to your boss on page 96.

Whether you need just the right sentiment for an anniversary, birth announcement, birthday greeting, get-well message, graduation, or any other milestone that you could care less about because it's happening to someone else, *The Official Compendium of Snark* will provide the perfect message.

I'm not making any age-related jokes because I genuinely feel bad about how old you are.

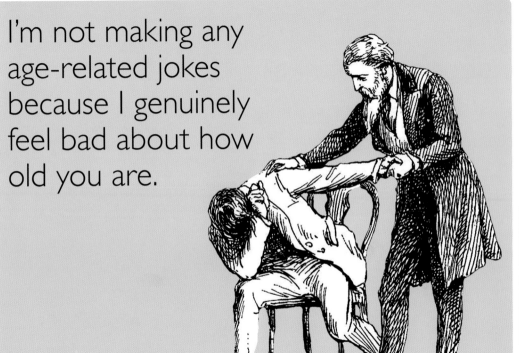

May your birthday be devoid of cute animals and soul-shredding wordplay.

May you live
long enough to
shit yourself.

B
I
R
T
H
D
A
Y

11

Today's the anniversary of you being expelled from your mother's uterus.

You've reached
an age that has no
significance at all.

Happy birthday to one of the few people whose birthday I can remember without a Facebook reminder.

I remember when you weren't so disturbingly old.

Let's over-celebrate
your birthday.

Even though we're
no longer sleeping
together, happy birthday.

Wishing you a
happy birthday
makes me
feel gay.

This is the perfect day to thank me for remembering your birthday.

I'd like to take you out for your birthday when it's convenient for me.

Congratulations on being a year closer to finding out if atheism was the right choice.

You'll never guess what I got you for your birthday because I didn't get you anything for your birthday.

Here's to another year of complete disregard for age-appropriate developmental milestones.

Let me know if you're leaving Facebook so I can say happy birthday for the last time ever.

Just wanted to be the first one to wish you a happy birthday so I can feel superior to your other well-wishers.

I'd be much more into your birthday if it was my birthday.

Sorry in advance for doing a ton of stupid shit.

Sorry for being myself.

APOLOGY

Sorry you don't understand how important I am.

Sorry you misinterpreted my brilliant joke as horribly offensive.

Congratulations on defying marriage statistics.

It's remarkable how long we've tolerated each other.

If I still had a soul,
you'd be its mate.

Happy anniversary to a couple who almost never makes me physically ill.

Happy anniversary from someone you're probably shocked knew it was your anniversary.

Here's to another year of staying together for the kids.

ANNIVERSARY

Let's celebrate the day you gave up on finding anyone better than me.

Congratulations on your new job that you probably won't like any better.

Congratulations on finding your true calling.

Congratulations on ending your dry spell.

Congratulations
on still having
most of your hair.

Congratulations on finding an absurdly overpriced place to live.

Congratulations on running a marathon without having to stop for a heart attack.

I hope a mediocre Mother's Day brunch can help negate 364 days of smug ingratitude.

I love how we don't even need to say out loud that I'm your favorite child.

Thanks for not ditching me in a dumpster.

Have a happy Mother's Day before your kids reach an age when they're completely jaded about Mother's Day.

You're going to be a great MILF.

I promise to come see the baby before it goes to college.

Congratulations on your new baby if it was intentional.

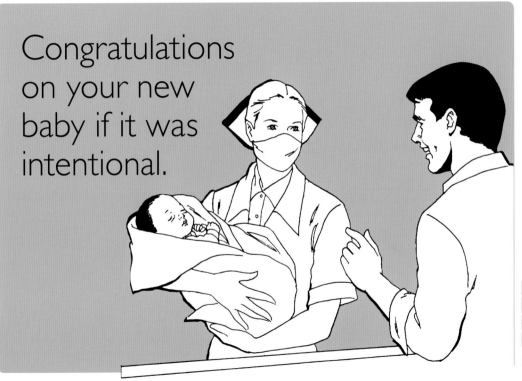

Dad, you've always been like a father to me.

Happy Father's Day to a wonderful husband who no matter what having kids has done to my body still seems to want to nail me.

You're the world's greatest dad although my frame of reference is limited.

Sorry you're feeling like such a pussy.

Get well soon because your cough is fucking disgusting.

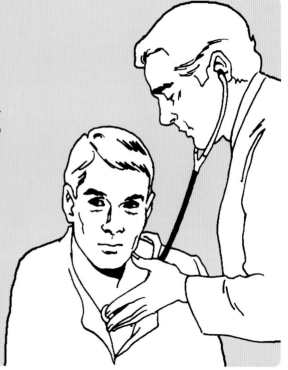

Get well soon
before the company
realizes you're
expendable.

Get well soon
so that I find you
attractive again.

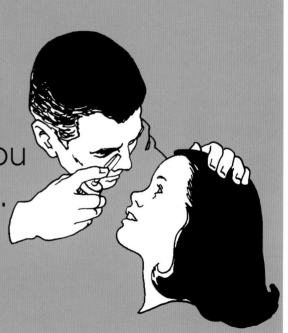

Maybe you'll start feeling better if you stop reading WebMD.

You just wasted up to $200,000.

May your college memories last as long as your student loan payments.

Just wanted to congratulate myself on sitting through your graduation ceremony.

Congratulations on four years of successfully pretending your safety school was your first choice.

I'm confident you'll succeed at any job that doesn't require drug testing.

Congratulations on sleeping with the same person for the rest of eternity.

Congratulations on probably not dying alone.

It would be
an honor to ruin
your wedding.

It's going to
be a great
first marriage.

Your wedding plans sound really interesting to you.

Congratulations on somehow not marrying the wrong person.

JUST HITCHED

Thanks for being a job reference despite what you know.

Thanks for returning my phone call with an email.

Thanks for always telling me which emerging buzz bands to have in my iPod.

I think of you every time I browse my cell phone on the toilet.

Wanted to touch base in case you get rich.

If I were ever
to shoot you,
it would just
be in the leg.

We're total fucking badasses.

I will be your friend
no matter what you
put inside your anus.

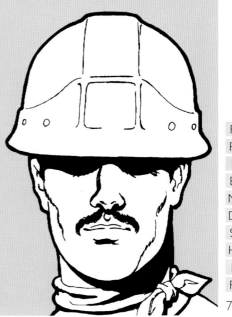

It's been too long since we threw up on each other.

Our effortless
friendship fits
perfectly with
my laziness.

If you ever disappeared while hiking, I'd remain with the search party until it started raining.

Let's talk soon because I miss you hearing the sound of my voice.

Just an FYI that you made it through my spring cleaning of Facebook friends.

I'd like to offer moral support but I have questionable morals.

When work feels overwhelming, remember that you're going to die.

Your new haircut looks great and exactly the same to me.

Get your shit together.

I'm outdoorsy in that I like getting drunk on patios.

My true love is out there somewhere and they can go fuck themselves.

I went to a better college than you.

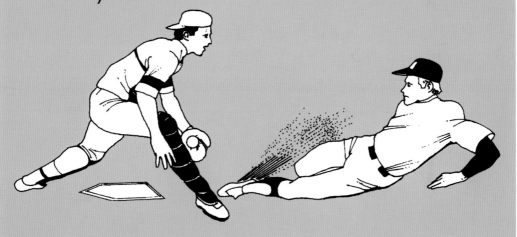

Just wanted to remind you how important it is to pay your taxes because they pay for my unemployment.

We're concerned your job is interfering with your drinking.

There are consequences to not doing your timesheets.

My sadness at your leaving the company is tempered by my excitement at taking your chair and computer speakers.

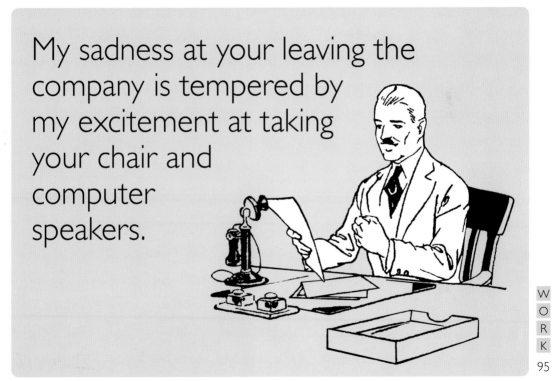

I've stopped even pretending to do anything around here.

Let's boost office morale by going out to drink and complain about office morale.

We're willing to do whatever it takes to keep you in this dead-end job.

Sorry I called, emailed, or IM'd you from three feet away.

Please stop
scheduling
Friday afternoon
meetings.

I couldn't get through Mondays without knowing you're equally miserable.

Let's spend countless hours preparing for a meeting that will be delayed, canceled, or misrepresented.

We've decided to change the name of the department in order to fix all its problems.

I'll be in late because I'm hungover or have a job interview.

I'm too busy to tell people how busy I am.

I deserve a raise for doing a half-assed job.

I can tell that you've pretended to work very hard on this project.

I think you misinterpreted the tone of my email.

Just getting on your radar because I may need something from you soon.

Appearing busy to avoid being laid off has become more exhausting than actually working.

You accidentally emailed me your darkest personal thoughts.

Sorry I accidentally cc'd you on an email insulting you.

Welcome to the company.

I send pointless emails late at night to impress coworkers.

I love pretending
I have the courage
to quit my job.

I can barely wait to take credit for your great ideas.

Let's factor my hangover into today's workload.

Your meeting is a high priority if there's free food.

Sorry your post-vacation workload has completely negated all the benefits of your vacation.

I own you.

I will be taking vacation precisely when you need me not to.

WORK
123

I or the company decided it's time for me to leave.

I could never replace you because it would be too costly and time-consuming.

Enjoy relentlessly panicking about what you're missing at work.

I'm already dreading having to look at your pictures.

FAREWELL

127

About the Authors

Brook Lundy is President, Head Writer, and Unpaid Intern of someecards.com. Before cofounding someecards, he was a copywriter in online advertising for over a decade, where his claim to absurd fame was the award-winning ShaveEverywhere.com Web site. He spent several years writing humor essays for publications such as *Details* and *The New York Times*, as well as writing and performing in a sketch comedy troupe.

Duncan Mitchell was born in New York and raised in San Francisco. He's been a package designer for The Clorox Company, an award-winning creative director in online advertising, and a peanut vendor at Candlestick Park. Currently he lives in New York where he is CEO, Assistant to the CEO, Art Director, and Junior Writer for someecards.com.

Contributors: Andrea Bichsel, Matt Cheplic, Jesse Darling, Sandy Dietrick, Andrew Kosow, Justin Laub, Danny Palmer, J. Courtney Sullivan, Jerry Tamburro